LIFE
IS
HARD

A GUIDED SELF-REFLECTION JOURNAL FOR TEENS

Making Sense of Life's Challenging Moments

Quote Usage Note
This journal includes selected inspirational quotations credited to their original authors. These brief excerpts are used under fair use for educational and inspirational purposes. The author and publisher do not claim ownership of these quotations. All rights remain with their respective copyright holders.

Published by Mindful Pathways Co., LLC
Printed in the United States of America
ISBN: 979-8-218-90825-6

Dedication

This first publication is dedicated to my firstborn son, Elijah—who constantly tests my patience and my parenting skills. The teen years really should come with a manual for us both, but until then, may this journal help guide you through life's storms. You were the inspiration for this project, and I hope it serves as a reminder of the strength, love, and resilience we both carry.

Author's Note

This journal is meant to be a space where you can slow down, reflect, and make sense of your thoughts, feelings, and experiences as you grow. There is no right or wrong way to use it. You can move through the pages in order, skip around, write a little or a lot, or simply sit with a question that matters to you.

This journal can be used on your own or alongside someone you trust. Some teens prefer to keep it private, while others find it helpful to share parts of it with a caregiver, parent, counselor, or mentor. Using this journal together can open conversations, build understanding, and create a sense of support.

For caregivers and parents, this journal is not meant to fix or rush growth. It is meant to encourage reflection, connection, and honest dialogue. Your role is to listen, ask thoughtful questions, and create a safe space for your teen to explore who they are becoming.

However it is used, the goal is the same: to support self-understanding, resilience, and growth.

Table of Contents

"Life doesn't get easier or more forgiving; we get stronger and more resilient."

— Steve Maraboli

Introduction

Life is hard. It's packed with highs, lows, and messy in-betweens that aren't always easy to figure out. Sometimes it feels unfair, confusing, or just plain overwhelming. But here's the thing: the most challenging moments often become the ones that shape us the most. They teach us lessons we can't learn when everything is smooth and easy. Hard seasons give us the chance to grow stronger, discover who we are, and figure out what we really care about.

That's why this journal exists. It's not here to give you all the answers or tell you who to be. It's here to help you slow down, notice what's going on inside, and make sense of your story. It's a place to reflect on your values, your identity, your friendships, and your future, so you can see more clearly who you are and who you want to become.

This journal is especially for anyone who doesn't always feel seen or understood. This journal was inspired by teens I've worked with over the years, many in foster care. What they wanted most—love, connection, purpose, and belonging—is the heartbeat behind these pages. Seeing their **resilience** and the **hope** they carried for the future, especially through the support of others (their community), helped me discover my own purpose. My hope is that these pages will help you discover yours, too.

> Journaling is pressing pause on the noise so you can hear your own voice.

Why Journaling Matters

Journaling is more than just writing on paper; it's a tool for healing, reflection, and growth. It gives you a safe place to release emotions, process experiences, and make sense of your past while imagining a better future. It helps you build insight into how your beliefs, choices, and goals shape the way you live, and it reminds you that your life has meaning, not only for yourself, but also in connection with others. In this way, writing becomes a quiet act of courage, a way to acknowledge pain and still choose growth.

What goal or hope do you have for yourself as you begin this journal?

_____

_____

_____

_____

Journaling is just one tool among many when it comes to processing your thoughts and emotions. The deep reflection questions in this journal may stir up strong feelings, and sometimes writing alone isn't enough. In those moments, you may find it helpful to reach out to a trusted friend or adult who can walk alongside you as you process. And if the weight of the world feels too heavy, I encourage you to reach out to a professional for additional support. We were never meant to go through life alone, and there is no shame in seeking help. In fact, humans tend to thrive when we connect with others. Our happiness, resilience, and hope grow stronger in community.

Creating a journal habit doesn't require perfection, just intention. Set aside a few minutes each day and let this be your space, free from pressure or judgment. At first, it might feel uncomfortable, and that's okay! Reflection takes practice. Journaling is like pressing pause on life. It helps you notice patterns in your thoughts and choices. *Writing things down can bring clarity when everything feels messy in your head, helping you see your thoughts more clearly and sort out what really matters.* You don't need to write perfectly. Doodles, bullet points, or half-finished sentences still count. What matters most is being honest with yourself and showing up consistently, even when the words feel hard to find.

Take Action: Make a 60-day commitment to this journal. A few minutes a day is enough to build the habit.

How to Use This Journal

- **One step at a time:** Pick one prompt a day. Sixty prompts = sixty days.
- **Be real:** Messy handwriting, crossed-out words, and spelling mistakes are welcome.
- **Dive deeper:** Each section includes activities to help you explore the big topics in a more hands-on way—so don't skip them!
- **Reflect often:** After every section, you'll find note pages. Use them to capture your thoughts, expand on your answers, or just let your ideas spill onto the page.
- **Have some fun:** Take advantage of the coloring pages sprinkled throughout.
- **Use the support tools:** Turn to **Key Ideas and Their Meaning** in the back of the journal to understand how emotions and ideas show up across these pages, using real examples and reflections rather than strict definitions.

Welcome to your story. Let's begin.

The Self: A Balanced Foundation

These stacked books represent the story of who you are. Like volumes placed one on top of another, your sense of self is built chapter by chapter, each part supporting and shaping the next. The bottom book, your identity, is the strong and steady foundation, and each book added above deepens your knowledge, experience, and growth. At the top rests your sense of purpose and meaning, guiding the narrative of your life.

This journal is designed around that idea. Each section builds onto the others, helping you explore how the different parts of your life connect and support one another. Every book matters. As you move through the pages, you will notice where your foundation feels strong and where you would like to keep writing and growing your story.

SECTION 1 — SELF & IDENTITY

> **"I am not what happened to me,
> I am what I choose to become."
> — Carl Jung**

Who Am I? Exploring Identity

Identity might sound like a hard-to-understand word, and even many adults struggle to describe their own identity. But really, it is just how you see yourself and the story you tell about who you are. It can feel tricky to put into words, or you might wonder what even counts as part of your identity. In the end, it all comes down to the pieces that make you, you. It is made up of your values, personality, interests, and how you fit into the world around you. **Values are especially important because they guide your choices, shape your goals, and reflect what matters most to you.**

Values often show up in different areas of life:

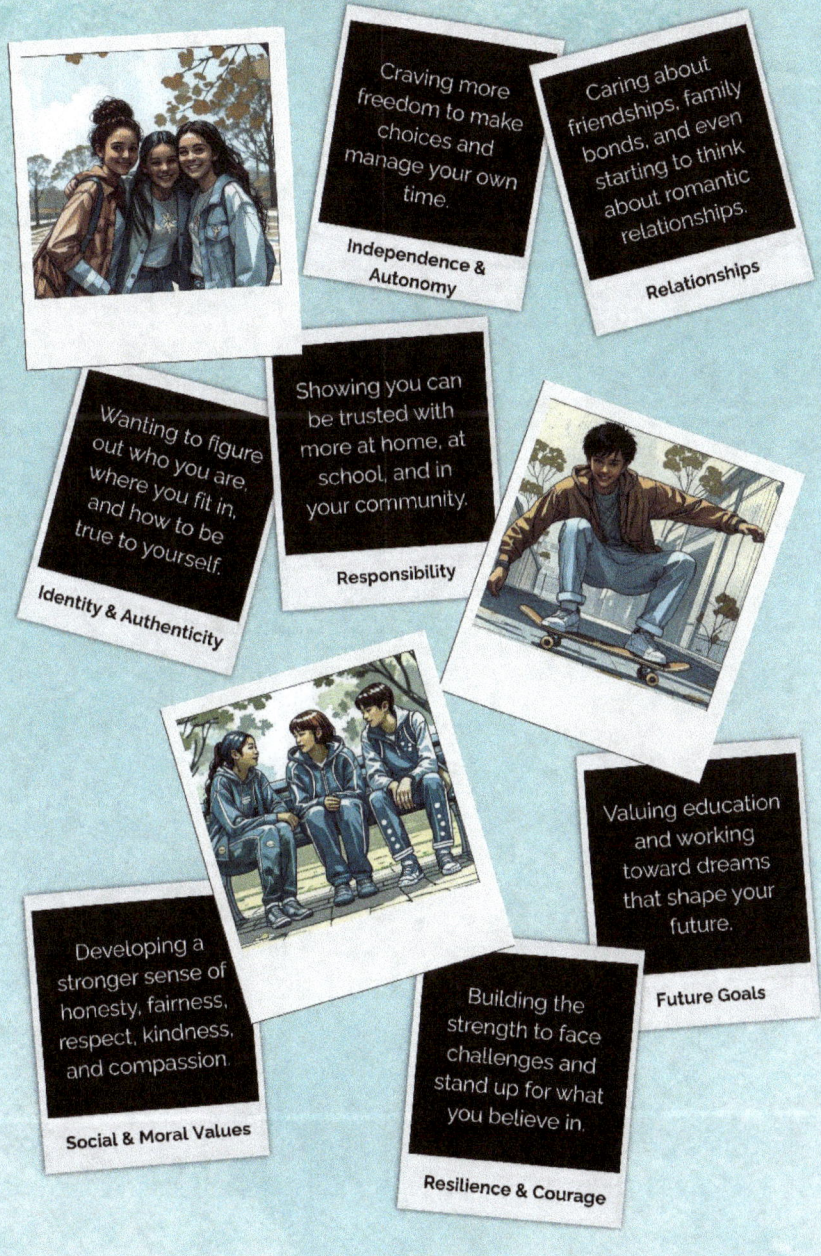

Craving more freedom to make choices and manage your own time.

Independence & Autonomy

Caring about friendships, family bonds, and even starting to think about romantic relationships.

Relationships

Wanting to figure out who you are, where you fit in, and how to be true to yourself.

Identity & Authenticity

Showing you can be trusted with more at home, at school, and in your community.

Responsibility

Valuing education and working toward dreams that shape your future.

Future Goals

Developing a stronger sense of honesty, fairness, respect, kindness, and compassion.

Social & Moral Values

Building the strength to face challenges and stand up for what you believe in.

Resilience & Courage

These values are like a compass. They point you toward the kind of person you want to be, even when life feels uncertain. And just like a story, your identity keeps developing. You are the author, and you get to decide how the chapters unfold.

> **You get to decide who you are and who you're becoming—one choice, one chapter at a time.**

Identity does not appear overnight. It starts in childhood, when parents, caregivers, and other people in your life show you what is expected and tell you things about yourself. Maybe you grew up being called shy, athletic, bossy, or funny. Some of those labels may still feel true, and some may not fit anymore. That is because identity is not fixed. As you grow, you get to question the old pieces, keep what feels real, and let go of what does not.

As you get older, you start to shape your identity for yourself. You can keep the parts that still feel right, change what no longer fits, and add new qualities that reflect your interests, values, and goals. Over time, this helps you grow into a version of yourself that feels more real and authentic.

Are there old labels or ideas about yourself that no longer fit?

As you figure out who you are, it's also important to think about reputation, which is how others see you based on your actions over time. **Reputation** is shaped by the things you do every day, like how you treat people, whether you keep your word, and how much effort you put into what matters to you. You can't control what everyone thinks, but you *can* decide how you want to show up and what kind of person you want to be known as. Over time, those choices reflect the kind of identity you're building and the values you live by.

Identity can show up in many ways:

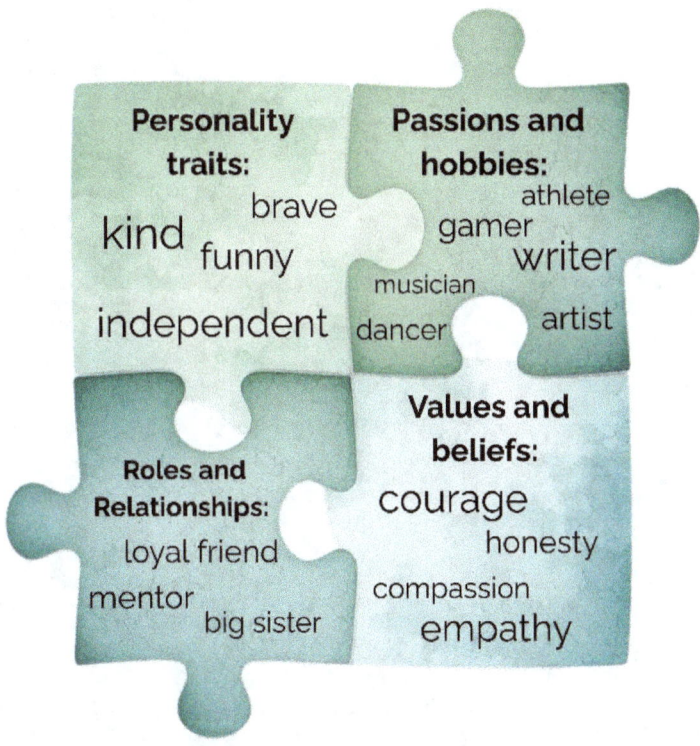

All of these pieces work together to create who you are right now, while still leaving space for growth.

Family and community are not the only things that shape identity. Life experiences play a huge role. Winning an award, joining a team, or making a close friend can add positive pieces to your story. Painful experiences can shape identity, too. Rejection, loss, or tough situations can leave a mark.

To get through hard times, many of us learn survival moves. Maybe you stayed quiet because speaking up felt like it would create more problems than relief, put others first to feel needed, or acted tough even when you were hurting inside. Those moves showed strength and helped you in the moment, but if you hold on to them for too long, they can start to hold you back.

For example:

Staying quiet can make it hard to speak up for yourself

Always putting others first can leave you drained

Acting strong all the time can stop you from asking for help

Part of growing into your true self is noticing which moves helped you survive and deciding if they still help you now.

Here is something else to remember when life is heavy: you have proof that you are strong. Every time you kept going through a hard day, learned from a mistake, or showed up when it would have been easier to quit, you added evidence to your worthiness. You can keep a journal of evidence—real moments that show you: I am capable, I am learning, and I kept going on days that were challenging.

> On hard days, you can use your journal to look back and remind yourself of what you are capable of. It becomes evidence that you are more than your struggles and that you have already overcome challenging moments.

Let's Practice: Building Your Evidence Journal

Think of a time you faced something really hard and made it through. Maybe it was something that tested your confidence, your patience, or your heart. Use the space below to reflect on what that moment taught you about yourself.

- **Challenge I faced...** _____
- **What I felt then...** _____
- **What helped me get through it...** _____
- **What I learned about myself...** _____
- **How I feel about it now...** _____

Why Having a Strong Identity Matters

If you don't take time to figure out who you are, life can feel confusing, like setting out on a trip without a map or a compass to guide you. Teens often face these struggles when a sense of self is shaky:

- **Feeling Lost:** copying others just to fit in, but still feeling disconnected.

- **Mental Health Struggles:** more anxiety, more sadness, and doubting yourself.

- **Relationship Problems:** harder to build healthy friendships or feel truly close to others.

- **Peer Pressure:** easier to go along with the crowd and do things that do not feel right.

- **Feeling Stuck:** not knowing what you want or who you want to become, which makes goals harder to set.

All of these pieces work together to create your identity: your traits, values, experiences, and roles. But identity is not just one thing. It is made of many connected parts that shift and grow over time. To see how these pieces fit together, you will explore the Five Sides of Me.

> **When you take time to understand yourself, life feels clearer. Your five sides connect like stars, guiding your path forward.**

Each side — Creative, Coping, Social, Essential, and Physical — gives you a different way to understand who you are and who you are becoming.

The next activity is a process, not a race. Take your time. You might come back to different sides on different days and notice new things each time. There is no rush. Let your reflections unfold naturally, the same way your identity does.

Activity: Exploring the Five Sides of Me

You are more than what shows on the surface. Your thoughts, feelings, talents, skills, and goals all come together to shape who you are. This activity helps you explore different sides of your identity and understand yourself better.

1. **Creative Self** – How you express yourself and use your talents, such as being funny, curious, artistic, or hardworking.
2. **Coping Self** – How you handle stress and challenges by managing emotions, using hobbies, and finding ways to stay calm.
3. **Social Self** – How you connect with others through love, friendship, and **belonging**, such as being a loyal friend or a team player.
4. **Essential Self** – Your deeper values, beliefs, culture, or spirituality, including fairness, faith, family traditions, and finding **meaning**.
5. **Physical Self** – How you care for your body through sleep, nutrition, movement, and self-care.

Which of the five sides do you connect with the most?

Creative Self

The **Creative Self** is the part of your identity that shows how you express yourself, how you think, and the unique talents or strengths you bring into the world. It's not just about being "artistic", it's about the different ways you show your personality, problem-solving, and imagination in everyday life.

This might look like:

- **Style & Appearance**: Choosing outfits that show your vibe, decorating your room, or experimenting with hair and makeup.

- **Hobbies & Talents**: Gaming, sports, TikTok trends, cooking, fixing things, helping others, music, dancing or learning something new.

- **Problem-Solving**: Finding ways to include everyone when friends cannot agree on plans, coming up with new ways to study for a test, or finding ways to make money to buy something important.

- **Humor & Personality**: Making people laugh with your jokes, creating memes, or being the one in your friend group who always finds a fun way to turn boring moments into something entertaining.

Style & Appearance

How do you express yourself through what you wear or how you design your space?

Hobbies & Talents

What is something you enjoy learning or want to get better at?

Problem-Solving

What's one challenge you've handled better than you thought you would?

Coping Self

The **Coping Self** is the part of you that helps you handle stress, tough emotions, and daily challenges. Being a teen comes with ups and downs, pressure, conflict with friends, family expectations, and changes in your body that affect your mood.

It might show up as:

- Taking a break with music, sports, or a favorite hobby when you're overwhelmed.

- Using humor to lighten the mood when things feel heavy.

- Talking things through with a friend or mentor instead of bottling it up.

- Learning healthier coping skills, like journaling, mindfulness, or breathing exercises.

Your Coping Self is your survival toolkit. Some coping habits help you grow, while others might only work short-term. The goal is to recognize what works best for you and keep building healthier strategies over time.

Learning and Using Coping Strategies

When life gets tough, whether it's friendship drama, family changes, or feeling like you don't belong, it's easy to feel stressed or overwhelmed. That's where coping strategies come in.

Coping strategies are the healthy tools and actions you use to handle stress, big emotions, or challenges. Think of them as your personal tool kit for mental health. They're the skills and habits that help you calm down, refocus, and work through hard feelings. Some are quick strategies (like taking a deep breath when you're nervous before a test), while others take more practice (like learning mindfulness, journaling, or building routines that keep you balanced).

Using healthy coping strategies is like strengthening your mental muscles. When you practice them, you're teaching your brain and body how to bounce back instead of getting stuck in worry, anger, or sadness.

Teens who build positive coping skills often notice:

>> Lower levels of stress and anxiety.

>> Better self-esteem and confidence.

>> Stronger friendships and relationships.

>> A reduced risk of depression and other mental health struggles.

When Would You Use Them?

When you feel overwhelmed by schoolwork, tests, or deadlines.

When a friend says or does something that hurts your feelings.

You feel frustrated, angry, or sad and are not sure why.

Without coping strategies, stress and disconnection can pile up, leading to feelings of hopelessness, irritability, or even withdrawal from friends and family. But with the right tools, you can take control of how you respond. Instead of stress controlling you, you're in charge. That shift can mean the difference between spiraling into negative thoughts and choosing a healthier path forward.

Each time you choose a healthy way to handle a difficult situation, you strengthen your ability to bounce back, adapt, and keep going. Coping helps you get through hard moments. **Resilience** is what grows because you did.

Let's Reflect:
When you are feeling overwhelmed, what do you usually do to cope right now? How does your body tell you when you are reaching your limit?

Coping Strategies

(Circle the ones you'd try or already use!)

 Journaling

 Spending time with pets

 Listening to music

 Getting outside in nature

 Moving your body (walking, sports, dance)

 Resting or napping

 Deep breathing / mindfulness

 Watching something funny

 Creative outlets (art, writing, music)

 Reading a book

 Talking to a trusted friend

 Having a calming routine (tea, shower, skincare)

 Asking for help (counselor, teacher, parent)

When I feel stressed, I usually...

A healthy way I'd like to cope better is...

One thing that helps me calm down is...

NOTES:

Social Self

The **Social Self** is all about connection. Humans are wired for relationships, and as a teen, friendships, family, and social groups play a huge role in shaping who you are. This side of you helps you figure out how to communicate, build trust, and feel a sense of belonging.

It might show up as:

Being a loyal, supportive friend whom others can count on.

Feeling proud of your role on a sports team, in a club, or in a faith or cultural community.

Learning to set boundaries when someone crosses the line.

Handling challenges in friendships, like conflict, jealousy, or peer pressure.

Your Social Self reminds you that identity isn't built alone. The way you connect with others helps shape how you see yourself, and healthy relationships can make you feel seen, valued, and supported.

A friend would describe me as...

A positive way I show up for the people in my life is...

One way I can be a better friend, sibling, or teammate is...

NOTES:

Essential Self

Your **Essential Self** is the deeper part of you, the side that carries your **values**, **beliefs**, and sense of purpose. These are the ideas that shape how you see yourself, others, and the world. They're like the "rules of life" you carry inside.

 Values...
are what you decide are most important to you (like honesty, loyalty, fairness, or safety).

 Beliefs...
are the thoughts you accept as true about yourself, people, or the world (like "I can trust others," or "I'm not good enough").

Even if you haven't thought about them much, values and beliefs quietly guide your feelings and decisions. They show up when you ask yourself, *"What matters to me? Who do I want to be? How do I want to treat others?"*

Your values influence how you treat others, how you handle problems, and how you make decisions.

For example, if you value honesty, you try to tell the truth even when it is uncomfortable. If you value loyalty, you show up for your friends and keep their trust. If you value respect, you speak up when something feels wrong and respect other people's boundaries. If you value effort, you keep trying at school or in activities, even when things do not come easily.

Take a moment to reflect: What experiences have helped shape what matters to you? What have they taught you about trust, love, or self-respect?

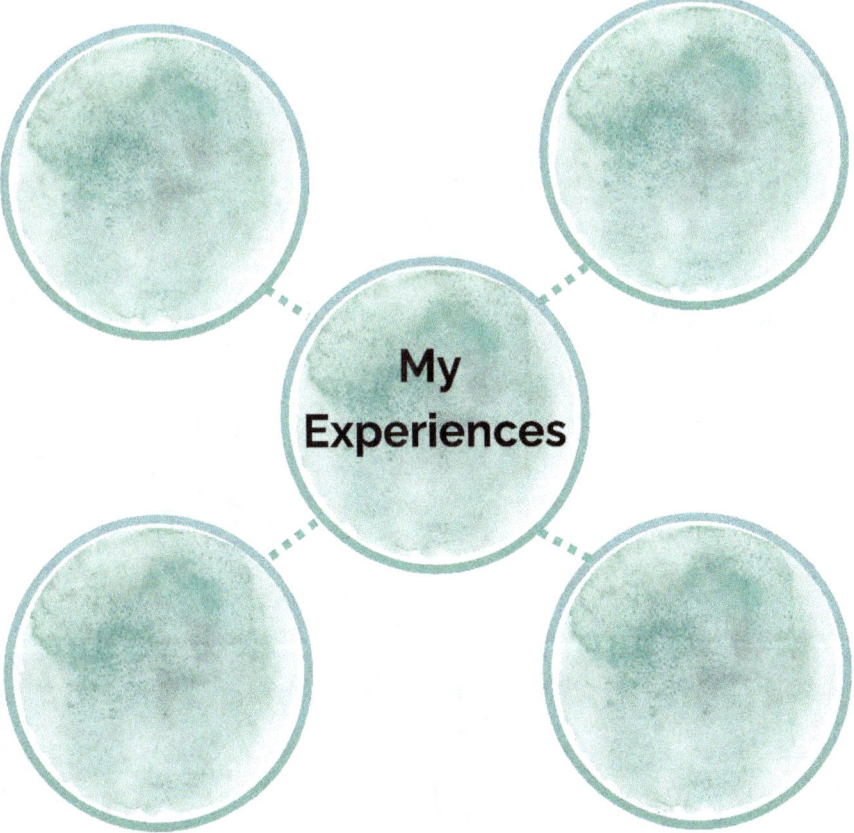

Hard or confusing experiences can shape how we see ourselves and others. Sometimes we carry beliefs that helped us get through those moments, even if they no longer fit who we are now. As you grow, you have the chance to let go of what no longer helps and choose beliefs and values that better support the life you want to build.

What beliefs did you tell yourself during a hard or challenging moment? Do those beliefs still support you today? For example, a belief like "I have to handle everything on my own" might have helped before, but a belief like "It is okay to ask for help" may support you better now.

Creating Healthier Values and Beliefs

The good news is that values and beliefs aren't permanent. They can grow, change, and be rewritten as you heal and discover who you truly are. Healthy beliefs and values give you strength, hope, and direction.

Here are some examples:

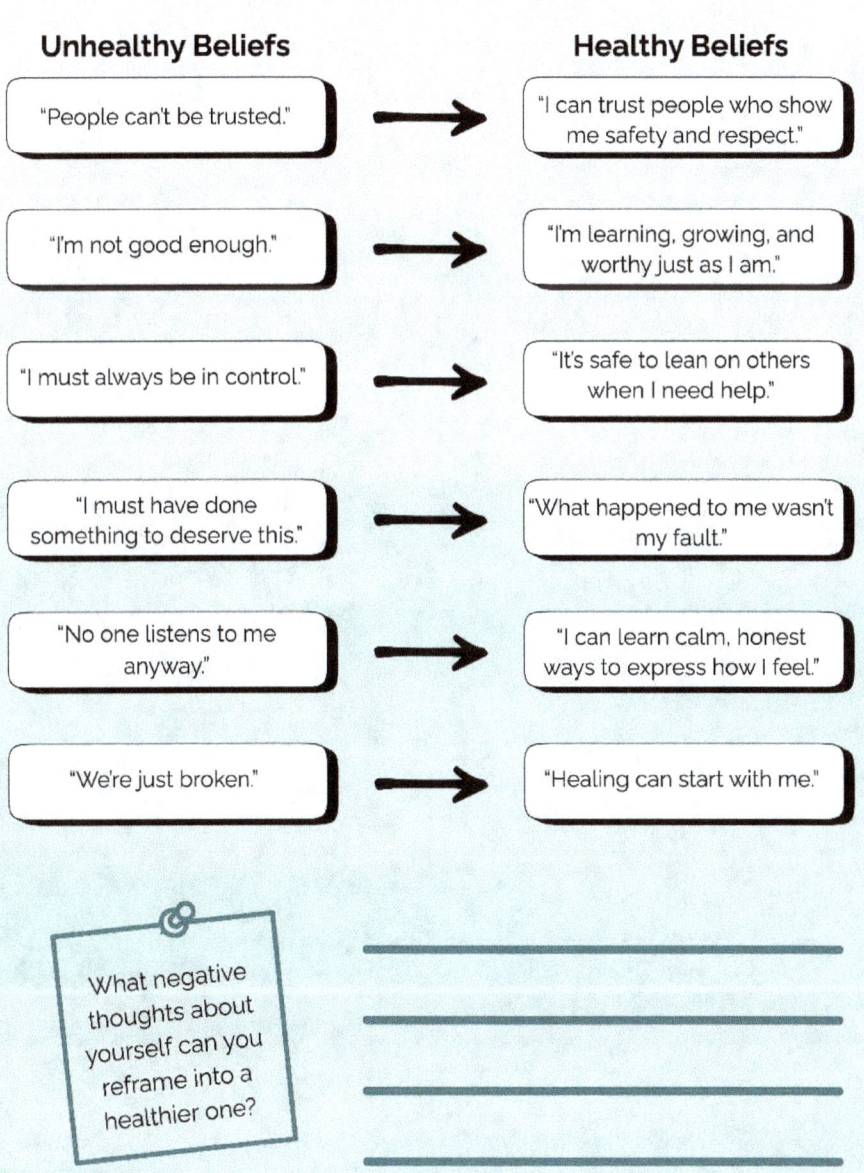

Unhealthy Beliefs

"People can't be trusted."

"I'm not good enough."

"I must always be in control."

"I must have done something to deserve this."

"No one listens to me anyway."

"We're just broken."

Healthy Beliefs

"I can trust people who show me safety and respect."

"I'm learning, growing, and worthy just as I am."

"It's safe to lean on others when I need help."

"What happened to me wasn't my fault."

"I can learn calm, honest ways to express how I feel."

"Healing can start with me."

What negative thoughts about yourself can you reframe into a healthier one?

_____

_____

_____

_____

A value or belief that matters most to me is...
(refer to pg. 25)

Something (or someone) that makes my life feel important
or special...

One tradition, routine, or habit I have that helps me feel
grounded or connected is...

NOTES:

The Physical Self is the part of your identity connected to your body, health, and energy. It includes how you take care of yourself physically, but it also affects how you feel emotionally and mentally. Your body and mind are connected, which means when one is struggling, the other often feels it too.

When your physical health is off, such as dealing with an injury, long term illness, or a new medical diagnosis, it can affect your mood, confidence, focus, and stress levels. Feeling tired, uncomfortable, or unwell can make everyday things feel harder. This does not mean something is wrong with you. It means your body is asking for care and support.

Taking care of your Physical Self is a way of showing self-respect. Fueling your body with nourishing food, moving in ways that feel good, and allowing yourself to rest all help support both your physical and mental health. Movement is not about changing your body. It is about helping your body release stress, build strength, and feel more balanced.

Your physical self gives you clues about what is going on inside you. Your body often communicates through energy levels, tension, and discomfort. Paying attention to these signals can help you understand what you need instead of ignoring how you feel.

Low energy can sometimes mean you need more rest or better sleep, but it can also mean your body needs movement. Being still for long periods can make you feel more tired. Headaches or eye strain after too much screen time may be your body asking for breaks, stretching, or fresh air. Feeling out of breath or struggling with basic exercise can be a sign that your body needs more regular movement or gentler ways to build strength.

Most teens benefit from about 60 minutes of physical activity each day. This does not have to be intense or athletic. Walking, biking, dancing, playing a sport, stretching, or moving your body in ways that feel good all count. Movement helps boost energy, improve mood, reduce stress, and support both physical and mental health.

How does staying up late on your phone affect your energy and focus the next day?

How do different foods impact your mood and energy?

How does your body feel when you move compared to when you sit for long periods?

How do rest, sleep, or downtime change how you feel physically and emotionally?

One thing I like about my body is...

A way I take care of myself physically is...

One small step I could take to feel healthier or stronger is...

Reflection Challenge

- Circle the area where you feel the strongest right now.
- Put a star next to the area you'd like to grow in the most

Action Plan: Turning Reflection into Growth

1. My Focus Area:

_____

2. One Small Step I Can Try This Week:

_____

3. How I'll Remember (reminder, note, friend, etc.):

_____

NOTES:

Reflection
Prompts

Recently, I felt most like my true self when...

How can I create more moments like this in my week?

A value I want to live by this week is... (refer to pg.25)

What small action can I take to show it in my daily life?

Something small I accomplished that deserves a fist bump is...

How does this connect to the kind of person I want to be?

When stress spiked, I coped by...

Did it really help, or is there a healthier way I could try next time?

A negative thought I noticed myself repeating was...

What could I tell myself instead that feels kinder and truer?

I showed self-respect by making a choice that felt right for me when I...

Where else in my life could I show up for myself more?

One decision I'm proud of today is...

How does this choice reflect the person I'm becoming?

If that mean little voice in my head had a name, it would be ___, and it usually says...

What could a more confident voice say instead?

An interest or hobby that makes me feel more like myself is...

How could I make more time for this or explore it further?

One habit I want to build or stop is...

If I stick with this change, how might it shape the kind of person I'm becoming?

My body showed signs of stress, like tension, headaches, stomach discomfort, restlessness, or feeling tired, when...

What might my body be asking for in that moment?

A song lyric, quote or famous saying that I connect with...

How does it connect to who I am or who I want to become?

SECTION 2 — FRIENDS & COMMUNITY

> "Connection is why we're
> here; it is what gives purpose
> and meaning to our lives."
> — Brené Brown

Finding Your People

Everyone needs connection. From the very beginning of life, our sense of safety and identity is shaped by the people and groups around us. As we grow, friendships, family, school, sports, clubs, and neighborhoods all create a web of relationships that helps us feel supported, valued, and less alone. Belonging is not just something extra; it is a vital part of overall well-being and identity.

But connection is not always easy. Friendships can bring out our best, but they can also stir up fears of rejection, **shame**, or not being enough. Sometimes it feels safer to stay quiet, hide parts of ourselves, or choose comfort instead of **courage**. Other times, misunderstandings or comparisons can leave us feeling left out or disconnected.

And sometimes the people closest to us might even encourage choices that do not align with our values. This could look like pressure to act tough, join in on gossip, break rules, or ignore our true feelings just to fit in. While it may feel easier in the moment, these patterns can pull us away from the person we really want to be.

These challenges are part of being human, and facing them helps us grow stronger, braver, and more **authentic** in our relationships — meaning we can show up as our real selves instead of pretending to be someone we are not. Learning to notice when connections lift us up and when they drag us down gives us the power to choose relationships that support the best version of ourselves.

When we find the courage to show up as our true selves, even when it feels risky, we create the chance for deeper trust and belonging. And when we recognize and appreciate the people who make us feel seen, we learn how powerful community really is.

When you think about the groups or friendships you are part of, when do you feel most included and supported, and when do you feel pressure to be someone you are not? What do those moments teach you about the kind of connections you want in your life?

What Is Community?

Community can mean many things. For some people, it is a friend group at school or online. For others, it is family, even with its ups and downs. Community may also be found in sports, faith groups, cultural traditions, art clubs, or neighborhood hangouts. In other words, community is the "who" and "where" of belonging: the people we trust and the places where we feel at home.

Community is also about **courage** — the courage to let ourselves be seen, to speak up when it is easier to stay quiet, or to admit we need support. True community is built not only on fun and shared experiences, but also on **honesty** and **vulnerability**.

> **When you dare to be real, you invite others to do the same.**

Vulnerability means showing our real selves, even when it feels scary. It might look like admitting we are nervous before a big game, sharing that we are having a tough day, or letting a friend know when we feel left out. Vulnerability also means being willing to sit with your own emotions instead of pushing them away or distracting yourself from them. It takes courage to notice what you are feeling and allow it to exist without judging it. *When was the last time you wanted to be honest about how you were feeling but hesitated?*

Vulnerability does not mean oversharing or telling everyone everything. It means trusting the right people with the real parts of us. When we take that risk, we give others permission to be real too, and that is where deeper connection happens. *Who in your life feels safe to be honest with, and what makes them feel trustworthy?*

It takes boldness to be vulnerable, but it is often the first step toward finding the kind of friendships and communities where we feel truly accepted.

Who Are Your People?

Write names, groups, or places in the circles where you feel supported or connected.

Challenges in Friendships and Community

Staying connected can be tough, especially during times of change and self-discovery. Some of the common struggles include:

Friendship Conflicts: Miscommunication, jealousy, or betrayal can strain friendships and make it tough to rebuild trust.

Life Transitions: Moving or new routines can disrupt our sense of belonging.

Social Comparison: Comparing ourselves to others can make us feel not good enough or afraid to be real.

Trust and Trauma: Past hurt can make trusting others feel risky, leading to isolation.

Feeling Different: Differences in culture, identity, or ability can create exclusion or misunderstanding.

Peer Pressure: Friends might encourage choices that do not match our values, challenging us to stay true to ourselves.

Why Belonging Matters for Mental Health

Everyone wants to feel like they fit in. When we do not feel connected, it is easy to feel lonely, anxious, or stuck in fear of rejection. But when we have good friends, supportive peers, or a community we feel part of, it makes a huge difference. These connections can help us handle stress, bounce back when life gets tough, and remind us that we are not alone.

For example:

- Having one trusted friend can give us the courage to face bullying.
- Being part of a community service club can help us feel purposeful and valued, even when family life feels unstable.
- Admitting we are struggling can sometimes bring deeper friendships instead of rejection.

Problems with Disconnection & Overuse of Social Media

Many people turn to social media and online spaces to feel connected. Platforms like TikTok, Instagram, group chats, and online gaming communities can offer a sense of belonging, especially for people who feel different, shy, or misunderstood in real life. Gaming can be a place where you feel skilled, valued, and part of a team. Social media can help you stay in touch, express yourself, or feel less alone. Those connections are real, and they matter.

At the same time, these spaces can quietly create new challenges. When you scroll through social media, it can seem like everyone else has perfect skin, perfect grades, perfect friendships, and perfect lives. In gaming spaces, it might feel like everyone else is always winning, ranking up faster, or performing better than you. It's easy to start comparing yourself and wondering why you don't measure up.

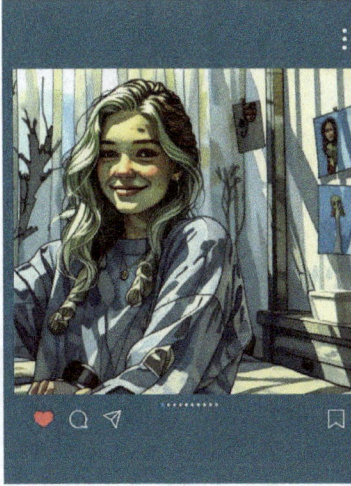

Here is the truth: no one's life is actually like that. What you're seeing online is a highlight reel, not the full story. People share wins, funny moments, and filtered snapshots, but not the stress, loneliness, mistakes, or self-doubt happening behind the scenes. Even the people who look confident online have off days, insecurities, and struggles you don't see.

Online spaces can be fun, creative, and connecting, but they are not meant to define your worth. Your value isn't measured by likes, followers, views, or game stats. Real confidence grows when you understand who you are beyond the screen and learn to notice how these spaces make you feel, not just how often you use them.

Let's Reflect: When you want to feel close to someone, where do you usually turn first — online or in real life? After spending time on social media, do you feel more connected... or more alone?

Real connection does not come from likes, views, or followers. It comes from being around people who accept you exactly as you are, even when you are not "picture perfect." Someone might spend hours online and look socially active, but still feel anxious when no one responds to their messages. Another person might find encouragement in an online group, but without support in real life, they may still feel alone.

Social media can easily lead to comparison and feelings of **shame** — that quiet voice that tells you "You are not enough," not interesting enough, not attractive enough, or not worthy of being seen. When shame settles in, it can make you feel invisible, disconnected, or like you have to become someone else to belong. While likes and comments may offer temporary comfort, they often lack real depth. You can feel plugged in and still feel empty at the same time.

Trust: With Ourselves and Others

Trust is the foundation of every healthy connection, but it does not always come easily. Trust has two parts: trusting ourselves and trusting others.

Trusting ourselves means believing that our feelings, thoughts, and needs are real and worthy of respect. Sometimes it is easy to second-guess ourselves because of comparison or pressure, but trusting ourselves means remembering that our story matters, even if it does not look picture-perfect.

Trusting others means taking the risk to let people in. It is choosing vulnerability, sharing a secret, admitting we are struggling, or showing the parts of ourselves we usually keep hidden. This can feel scary because it opens the door to possible rejection or betrayal. But without that risk, relationships stay shallow, and we miss out on the deeper bonds that make us feel truly seen and supported.

Trust often requires courage over comfort. It is more comfortable to hide, pretend, or stay silent, but real trust grows when we step into **honesty**.

Trusting ourselves might look like setting a boundary, even if it feels awkward, because honoring our needs matters.

 Trusting others might look like admitting we are nervous before a big game, and realizing our friend encourages us instead of laughing.

For those who have experienced rejection, betrayal, or trauma, trust can feel especially difficult. It is natural to want to protect ourselves by shutting people out. But healing often starts with small steps, testing the waters with safe people, honoring our own voice, and reminding ourselves that not everyone will let us down.

In the end, trust is not about being perfect or never getting hurt. It is about learning to balance caution with openness, protecting our hearts while still letting ourselves experience the closeness that comes from connection. Trust grows little by little, and each step builds the foundation for stronger friendships, healthier communities, and a deeper sense of belonging.

Think about a time when you wanted to trust but felt unsure. What made you hesitate? Was it fear of being judged, left out, misunderstood, or hurt again?

_____

Now think about a person in your life who feels safe. What makes them feel different? How do they speak to you? How do they show they care? How do you feel when you are around them?

_____

What Are Boundaries

Boundaries are like invisible lines that show where we end and someone else begins. They help us decide what feels safe, what feels respectful, and how we want to be treated. Boundaries are not about shutting people out; they are about letting people in at a pace that feels right.

Social media can sometimes blur these lines, making it seem like everyone deserves access to our time, attention, or personal life. But just like we would not let the whole world walk into our room uninvited, we do not have to let the online world decide our value. Setting boundaries means choosing what parts of ourselves we want to share, when, and with whom — both in real life and online.

Healthy boundaries are not walls; they are like doors. We get to decide when, how, and with whom we open them. Setting boundaries does not make us mean or difficult. It shows we respect ourselves, and it teaches others how to respect us too.

How Do Boundaries Help?

They protect our well-being (emotional, mental, and physical).

They give us permission to say "no" when something does not feel right.

They remind others of what is okay and not okay with us.

They make space for relationships that are built on respect, care, and honesty.

"Not everyone earns a front-row seat in your life"

When Might You Use Boundaries

When someone makes jokes that hurt our feelings.

When a friend pressures us to do something that goes against our values.

When we need alone time to recharge, even if others want our attention.

When we are sharing personal things and want to go at our own pace.

Activity: Setting Boundaries

There are times when we say yes even though we really want to say no. Maybe we don't want to disappoint someone, start drama, or look "mean." Boundaries help us protect our time, energy, and well-being. Saying no is not selfish. It is healthy. Think of a time when you agreed to something you didn't want to do. Use the steps on the next two pages to rewrite that moment in a way that protects you. Practice these steps as many times as you need. Setting boundaries takes lots of practice.

Step 1: Spot the situation

What felt uncomfortable or not okay for me?
One time I said yes when I wanted to say no was when...

_____

_____

Step 2: Identify your need

What would have helped me feel respected, safe, or comfortable? I would have felt better if...

_____

_____

Activity: Setting Boundaries

Step 3: Create a boundary statement
Use this sentence to show what you need next time:
"When _____ happens,
I need _____."

Step 4: Practice short phrases
Try saying one of these boundary lines out loud or in your head:

• "Please don't _____"

• "I'm not comfortable with that."

• "I can't today."

• "That doesn't work for me. Let's try _____ instead."

What if Someone Doesn't Respect my Boundaries!?

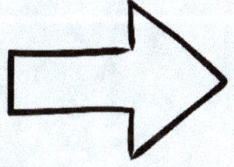

If Someone Doesn't Respect Your Boundaries...

Sometimes you can explain a boundary clearly and the other person still ignores it. That does not mean you did something wrong. Setting a boundary is only the first step. What matters next is how you take care of yourself. If someone does not respect your boundary, you still have options:

1. You can repeat your boundary calmly.
You do not have to explain or defend it again. Saying it clearly shows that your needs matter.

2. You can change what you do to protect yourself.
This might mean stepping away, limiting contact, muting messages, or choosing not to engage. Boundaries are about what you will do to stay safe and respected.

3. You can ask for support.
Talking with a trusted friend, parent, teacher, or counselor can help you feel supported and figure out what to do next.

4. You can choose distance if you need it.
Protecting your space, energy, and well-being is not mean. It is an act of self-respect.

Setting boundaries is not about controlling others. It is about taking care of yourself. If someone cannot respect your boundaries, you are allowed to decide how much access they have to you.

NOTES:

Reflection
Prompts

A moment I stayed quiet or went along with something to avoid being judged was...

How did I respond, and what would courage have looked like instead?

A time I ignored my own needs to keep the peace was...

How would I have felt if I had honored my needs instead?

I worried people wouldn't accept me when...

What does this fear say about what I value most in friendships?

A time I felt left out or misunderstood was...

What can I do differently next time to handle those feelings in a healthy way?

Something I appreciate about my friends, family, or community is...

How can I show gratitude or give back to them this week?

When I think about my closest friend, one quality I admire is...

How can I practice or grow that same quality in myself?

Something I hide about myself in friendships is...

What would it feel like to be fully seen and still accepted?

After spending time with certain people, my energy feels...

What boundaries or choices could help me protect my energy?

An activity, group, or club that helps me feel connected is...

What's one new opportunity I could try to grow my community?

When I compare myself to others, I sometimes believe...

What is a kinder, truer story I could tell myself instead?

A part of my story or identity that matters to me is...

How can I celebrate or share this part of myself more openly?

One way I'd describe the "vibe" of my friendships right now is... (calm, fun, stressful, supportive, etc.)

What kind of vibe do I want to create moving forward, and what's one step toward it?

SECTION 3 — LOVE & RELATIONSHIPS

> "We accept the love we
> think we deserve."
> — Stephen Chbosky

Building Your Foundation for Love

Relationships can feel exciting and confusing all at once. They can bring joy, closeness, and laughter, but they can also stir up questions and uncertainty. At the heart of it all, learning to love and value yourself is just as important as figuring out how to love someone else. **Self-love** is not about being perfect or obsessed with yourself. It means treating yourself with the same care, patience, and respect that you would give someone you truly care about. A positive relationship with yourself is what sets the tone for every other connection. The stronger your **self-love**, the clearer your expectations for how others treat you.

Loving yourself teaches others how to love you.

The foundation of who we are grows from understanding our identity, our experiences, and what matters to us most. Our identity is shaped by knowing our strengths, our story, and the choices we want to make about who we are becoming. These things guide how we show up in relationships and how we decide what feels right or wrong for us.

Our values and beliefs act as an anchor. They keep us grounded during hard moments and help us stay true to ourselves when emotions run high or situations feel overwhelming. When you are clear about who you are and what you stand for, your relationships are more likely to be built on confidence, stability, and purpose. This strong inner base shapes how you give and receive love.

> **A strong sense of self is the strongest relationship you'll ever build.**

Without a strong identity, relationships can feel confusing. You might find yourself bending to fit other people's expectations or accepting treatment that doesn't match what you truly deserve.

And when **self-love** is missing, it becomes even easier to tolerate relationships that don't meet your needs. Instead of feeling supported, you may end up feeling unseen, unappreciated, or less fulfilled. But when you build self-love, you raise the standard for what you allow into your life—you learn to expect respect, kindness, and care, both from yourself and from others.

What does love look like or feel like for me?

Love is not an object you can hold. It shows up in actions, words, and choices. Relationships aren't about finding someone to "complete" you; they're about sharing your life while still being fully yourself. The stronger your foundation of self and values, the easier it becomes to practice self-love, to set healthy expectations, and to build relationships that help you grow rather than shrink.

What Does Healthy Love Look Like?

Not everyone grows up seeing what healthy love looks like. Some people only see silence, arguing, distance, or relationships that feel tense or unsafe. So, if you have ever wondered what "normal" is supposed to look like, you are not behind. You are learning in real time, just like everyone else.

Sometimes the clearest signs of whether a relationship is healthy show up in your body, not your thoughts. Do you feel calmer after talking to someone or drained? Do you feel respected or small? This is where intuition comes in. **Intuition** is that quiet inner feeling that lets you know when something feels right, off, safe, or heavy, even if you do not have the words yet. When you spend time around someone who cares for you, your body often feels more relaxed, not more tense.

> Do the people in your life make you feel safe to be yourself, or do you feel like you have to change to be accepted?

Healthy connections make room for you, not shrink you. They allow space for different moods, perspectives, and stages of growth, without fear of rejection. You are not pressured to change, rush, or become someone else to be accepted. This section will help you recognize what support

actually feels like, and also notice when something does not. You deserve relationships that do not confuse your worth, silence your voice, or make you feel like love has to be earned.

Communication is a big part of a healthy relationship. It means not only talking but also listening and trying to understand each other. In good relationships, people feel safe saying what they think and feel, even when it is not easy. Problems are talked through calmly instead of yelling, shutting down, or trying to win. Good communication also means checking in with each other, asking questions, and making sure both people feel heard.

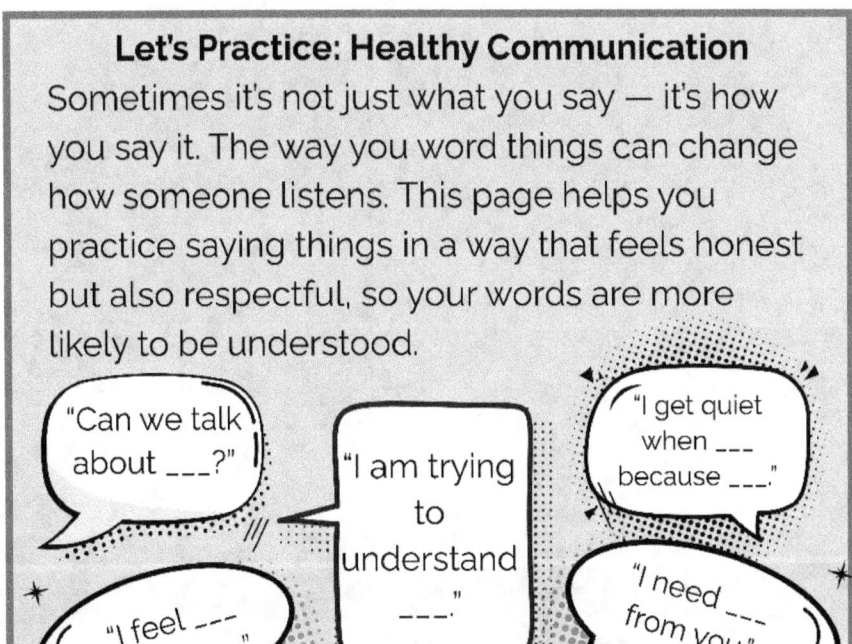

Let's Practice: Healthy Communication
Sometimes it's not just what you say — it's how you say it. The way you word things can change how someone listens. This page helps you practice saying things in a way that feels honest but also respectful, so your words are more likely to be understood.

"Can we talk about ___?"

"I am trying to understand ___."

"I get quiet when ___ because ___."

"I feel ___ when ___."

"I need ___ from you."

A healthy relationship does not take over your life. You still get to make your own choices, have your own goals, and spend time with the people who matter to you. Being in a relationship should not mean giving up your personality, your interests, or your voice.

In healthy love, you are free to be yourself. You are not controlled, tracked, or pressured to change who you are. You feel safe being honest instead of worried about getting judged or punished. The right relationship supports your independence and encourages you to grow into who you are meant to be.

When Love Doesn't Feel Healthy

Along with the signs of healthy love, it is also important to notice situations that do not feel right. Not every relationship or friendship is meant to last, and sometimes the biggest sign that something is wrong is how it makes you feel. If you often feel anxious, embarrassed, pressured, or unhappy around someone, that matters.

Love should not leave you hurting inside.

Some examples of unhealthy behavior include being told who you can talk to, feeling bad about how you look, being teased in a hurtful way, or having your feelings ignored. It can also show up as constant jealousy, pressure to move faster than you want, or always being the one who tries to fix problems. When a relationship feels one-sided, confusing, or uncomfortable most of the time, that is not healthy love.

Noticing these things does not mean you did something wrong. It just means you are learning what works for you and what does not. You deserve relationships that make you feel safe, respected, and supported.

Think about a time when someone did not treat you with care or respect. What did you notice about how your body reacted in that moment?

Building Self-Love & Self-Respect

Healthy relationships grow out of a healthy connection with yourself. **Self-love** is not arrogance or selfishness; it is valuing who you are, knowing you deserve respect, and taking care of your own needs and feelings. **Self-respect** means believing your needs matter and refusing to accept treatment that hurts, disrespects, or shrinks you. It is not just bubble baths, facemasks, or "treating yourself" (though

those can be fun parts of it). Real **self-love** shows up in how you talk to yourself, how you protect your energy, and how you honor your needs.

Self-love might mean choosing friends who respect you instead of pressuring you, speaking kindly to yourself after a mistake instead of tearing yourself down, or doing something that makes you feel proud, like finishing homework, practicing a sport, or learning a new skill. *Which of these comes most easily to you, and which feels hardest right now?*

It can also look like saying no when you do not have the energy to hang out, or when something feels wrong, even if that choice feels uncomfortable at first. Self-love often asks you to listen to your inner signals instead of ignoring them. *When was the last time your body or emotions tried to tell you something, and did you listen?*

Other times, self-love is quieter. It is caring for your body with rest, food, and movement, or giving yourself permission to feel your emotions instead of bottling them up. Accepting mistakes as part of growth, setting boundaries that show your needs matter, and surrounding yourself with people who remind you of your worth are all ways that self-love becomes visible.

When you practice self-love, you raise the standard for how others are allowed to treat you. Without it, it is easier to settle for relationships that leave you unseen or unappreciated. With it, you carry yourself with quiet confidence that says, I know my value, and I deserve respect. Self-love is the foundation, but **emotional safety** is what allows those relationships to grow. It is not enough to know your worth; you also need space and people who honor that worth.

> ## How I treat myself teaches others how to treat me.

♡ · Self-Love in Real Time · ♡

1. One way I take care of myself (not just physically):

_____

2. One choice I made (or want to make) that shows self-respect:

_____

3. Something I'm proud of myself for:

_____

4. One thing I need more of right now (rest, honesty, space, kindness, support, etc.):

_____

5. One boundary I want to practice setting:

_____

Emotional Safety

Emotional safety means being around people who make you feel accepted and comfortable being yourself. You should not feel afraid to speak up, hide parts of who you are, or change just to keep someone happy. *When you think about the people in your life, who helps you feel most like yourself, and why?*

You know a relationship feels emotionally safe when you can talk about your feelings without being laughed at, ignored, or punished for being honest. This might look like a friend who listens and keeps your trust, a partner who respects your limits, or an adult who takes what you say seriously and supports you. *How do you usually feel after opening up to someone — supported, relieved, or more tense?*

When emotional safety is present, relationships feel calmer, steadier, and more real. Trust grows more easily, and you feel free to be your true self without fear.

Activity: Emotional Safety Check-In

Instructions:

On a scale of 1 to 10, rate how emotionally safe you feel in your relationships (with friends, family, or a partner). Do this for each person.

1 = I rarely feel safe to be myself.

10 = I always feel safe, accepted, and supported.

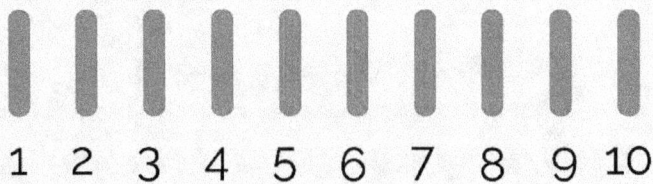

1   2   3   4   5   6   7   8   9   10

Once you've chosen your number, reflect on these questions:

- What situations, words, or actions make me feel **safer**?
- What situations, words, or actions make me feel **less safe**?
- Do I notice **patterns** in how certain people make me feel when I am around them?
- What could I do (or ask for) to feel **more emotionally safe**?

_____

_____

_____

_____

_____

_____

Green Flags & Red Flags
Checklist

🟩 **Green Flags** (Healthy Relationships)	🟥 **Red Flags** (Unhealthy/Toxic Relationships)
Consistent respect for your boundaries	Ignoring or pushing past your boundaries
Open and honest communication	Dishonesty, hiding things, or manipulation
Mutual effort and support	One-sided effort or control
Feeling safe to express emotions	Walking on eggshells or fearing their reaction
Encouragement of your goals and growth	Jealousy, competition, or holding you back
Taking accountability and apologizing	Blaming you for everything
Shared joy, laughter, and trust	Constant tension, criticism, or suspicion
Healthy independence and personal space	Possessiveness or isolation from others

(Tip: Circle or check the traits that show up in your relationships. Notice patterns.
Ask yourself: Am I choosing connections that nourish me, or ones that drain me)

NOTES:

Reflection Prompts

A moment when I felt loved...

What did that moment teach me about the kind of love I need?

I show that I care for someone by...

How did it affect the other person, and how did it affect me?

A tough conversation I handled (or avoided) was...

What can I learn about my communication style from this?

Something that makes me feel emotionally safe is...

Who in my life provides this feeling most consistently?

A time I noticed jealousy when I compared myself to someone else or felt like I was missing out...

What deeper need or fear might be hiding beneath it?

The way I show love best is ___, and the way I feel love best is ___

How can I communicate this clearly in my relationships?

One family or cultural tradition that matters to me (examples: holidays, game nights, religious practices, or special routines) is...

How does it connect to my values or sense of identity?

I practiced forgiveness (or need to) about...

How might forgiveness help me move forward or feel lighter?

A boundary that protects my heart is...

How can I reinforce this boundary without guilt?

I felt disconnected from those that I love when...

What is one small step I can take to repair or rebuild connection?

A role model for healthy relationships is...

What qualities or actions of theirs could I practice in my own life?

One habit that helps me feel good about myself is...

How does this habit help me show up better for the people I care about?

SECTION 4 — SCHOOL, WORK & FUTURE

> "The future depends
> on what you do today."
> — Mahatma Gandhi

Looking Ahead with Purpose

Your vision for the future is more than a dream; it is the picture you carry of who you want to become. The choices you make today are building blocks of the person you are becoming. This means realizing school is not just about grades, work is more than a paycheck, and preparing for the future helps build confidence and purpose.

But your vision does not stand alone. It is built on the foundation of your identity, strengthened by supportive relationships, and shaped by how you treat yourself with respect. Together, these pieces form the bigger picture of who you are becoming.

Becoming yourself is a long-term project.

School: More Than Just Grades

School is not only about homework and tests; it is a place where you practice the skills that help you succeed in life. Beyond memorizing facts, you are also learning creativity, problem-solving, and confidence through effort and practice. It comes with pressure, stress, and routines that can feel overwhelming at times. When school feels overwhelming, have you ever paused to ask yourself what skills you are actually building beneath the surface?

There are also setbacks: a grade lower than expected, not making a team, being left out, or missing an opportunity you worked hard for. These moments hurt because they challenge your belief in yourself. It is easy to compare yourself to others and think you are falling short. When something does not work out, do you see it as proof you are not enough, or as information you can learn from?

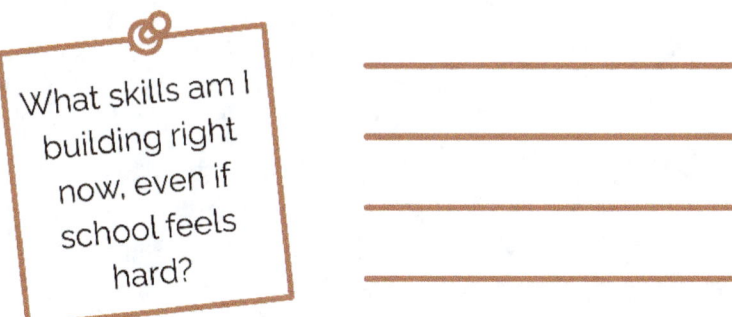

What skills am I building right now, even if school feels hard?

Here is the truth: setbacks do not define you. They usually mean you are learning through experience, not falling behind. A lot of people you see as successful today did not start out that way.

Billie Eilish was told her music was too quiet and different to succeed, and she was often dismissed early on. She kept creating anyway and became one of the youngest artists to win multiple Grammy Awards. MrBeast spent years making videos that barely got any views. Most people would have quit, but he kept experimenting, learning, and improving until his work finally took off.

What strengths have you noticed, even if they are still a work in progress? (For example: persistence, patience, problem-solving, asking for help, handling disappointment, or trying again)

Failure is not the opposite of success; it is part of it. And sometimes the bigger risk is not failing but never trying at all. Failure stings in the moment, but regret can last much longer. Think of school like learning to ride a bike. Each

assignment, sports practice, or project is another chance to show up and try. You may struggle at first, miss a shot, or not get the result you hoped for, but every attempt helps you learn what works and what does not. Over time, you build confidence and are better able to handle bigger challenges without losing momentum.

When you face challenging moments...

Pause and notice the feeling. Naming it makes it easier to move through.

Challenge the voice in your head. Replace "I am not smart enough" with "This one grade does not define me."

Look for the lesson. Ask, "What can I take from this to help me next time?"

Lean on support. A reminder from someone who believes in you can shift your perspective.

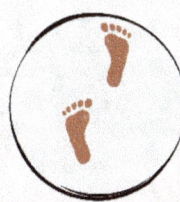

Keep moving forward. Even small steps — studying a little more, trying again, or exploring a new interest.

DONUT STOP TRYING

Work: Building Responsibility & Purpose

Work usually means a job with a paycheck, but it also includes everyday responsibilities like babysitting, chores, volunteering, or playing on a team. Each role, no matter how small, teaches you something about yourself. Babysitting might reveal patience, stocking shelves could sharpen focus, and being on a team can strengthen leadership.

These early experiences are practice rounds. They help you discover what excites you, notice your strengths, and recognize what does not fit.
Of course, any work brings challenges. You may have to stick to routines, manage time, or cooperate with people who see things differently. Mistakes will happen, like forgetting a task or responsibility or saying the wrong thing. Other times, you might feel rejected or overlooked.

These prompts help you reflect on the skills and strengths you are building through responsibilities, roles, and everyday experiences that prepare you for work and life.

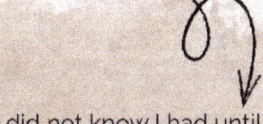

A strength I did not know I had until I had to show up or follow through:

_____

A role or responsibility that pushes me outside my comfort zone:

_____

Skills I am building that will help me in a job or future career:

_____

Some qualities that make someone dependable and successful include:

Reliability: showing up when you said you would.

Responsibility: taking ownership even when a task is difficult or dull.

Responsibilities, whether at home, school, or in the community, are less about perfection and more about discovery. They help you see what inspires you, highlight hidden strengths, and connect you to the people around you.

Positive attitude: putting in effort and choosing to see challenges as growth opportunities.

Teamwork: listening, communicating, and supporting others.

Adaptability: staying steady when plans shift.

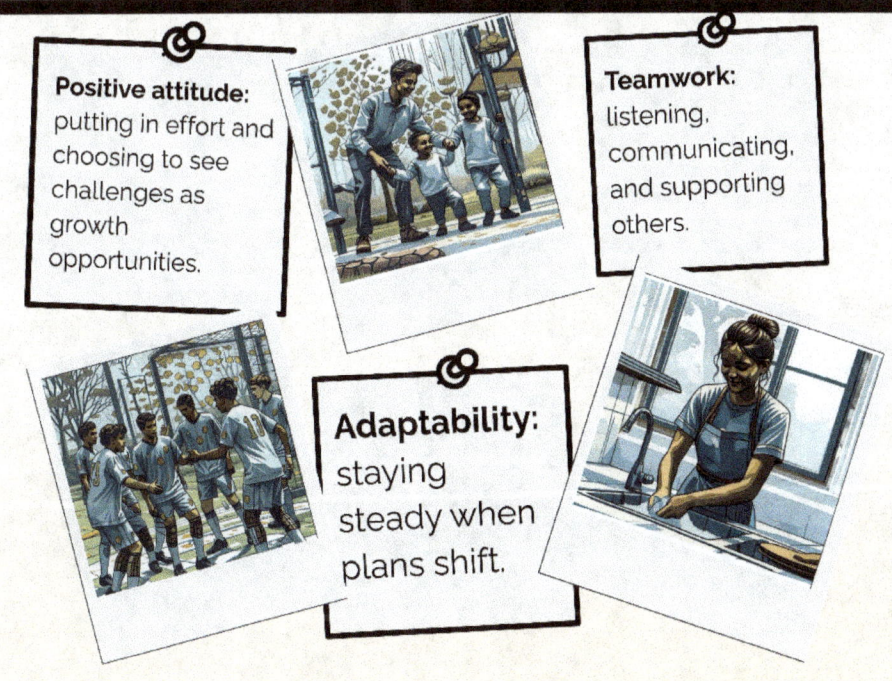

You may have noticed the word **resilience** come up a few times throughout this journal. Now is a good moment to slow down and really understand what it means.

Resilience is the ability to keep going when things do not go as planned. It is not about being tough all the time or pretending things do not hurt. It is about learning from hard moments, adjusting when something does not work, and choosing to move forward anyway, even when you are unsure of the next step. In those moments, it can help to pause and ask yourself what this experience might be teaching you, rather than judging yourself for getting it wrong. These moments are not wasted. They are lessons in resilience. They teach you how to listen to feedback, adapt when things change, and bounce back after a misstep. Being open to guidance does not make you weak; it shows maturity and a willingness to grow. Resilience is built over time, through effort, mistakes, support, and self-respect.

>>> **Getting back up counts more than getting it perfect.**

Each time you try again, ask for help, or choose not to give up on yourself, you are strengthening resilience, even if it does not feel that way in the moment.

Activity: Resilience Reset

Step 1: Name it
Write one challenge, setback, or hard moment you've dealt with recently.

_____

Step 2: Notice it
What made this hard was...

_____

Step 3: Find the response
Even though it was hard, I showed resilience by... (for example: trying again, asking for help, taking a break, staying calm, or not giving up).

_____

Step 4: Moving forward
Next time something hard comes up, one thing I can remind myself is...

_____

Future: Holding a Vision of What Is Ahead

Thinking about the future is really about exploration. It is about trying new things, noticing what fits, and learning about yourself along the way. But trying something new is not always easy. It can bring nerves, uncertainty, and questions that feel heavy. What if I fail? What if I pick the wrong thing? What if I am not enough?

The truth is, no one has it all figured out—not as a teen, and not even in adulthood. The future is not one perfect choice. It is a series of experiments. You try, you learn, and then you decide what to keep, what to let go of, and what to try next.

> **Small responsibilities build big skills.**

Even when you think you know what you want, your direction may change. That is not failure, it is growth. You might be sure you will be an athlete and later discover art or start chasing one career and realize another excites you more. Life is not about getting it right on the first try. It is about staying open, curious, and willing to adapt.

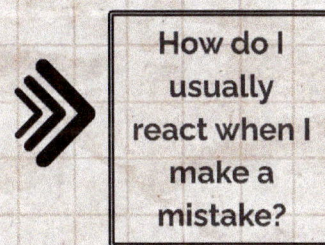

How do I usually react when I make a mistake?

Your choices do not have to define you forever. They are building blocks of your story, shaping your confidence, your skills, and your sense of purpose over time. What matters most is not being perfect; it is having the courage to take the next step, even when you feel uncertain or unsure of how things will turn out. In moments of doubt, it can help to pause and ask yourself what this choice might teach you about who you are becoming, rather than worrying about whether it is the "right" one.

Think of your future like a garden. Every choice, no matter how small, is a seed. Some seeds sprout quickly, like trying a new hobby and discovering you love it. Others take longer, like building trust, learning a skill, or developing confidence. Not every seed will grow into a tree, and that is okay. What matters is that you keep planting. Over time, those small seeds develop into lessons, skills, and confidence that quietly guide your path forward.

Try Something New

New experiences can feel exciting, scary, or both at the same time. They help you learn more about yourself, discover hidden strengths, and grow confidence in ways you might not expect. Every "yes" to something new adds another piece to your story. Here are some suggestions to get you started:

Plan a hike with family	**Join a local tournament**
Comic Drawing	**Volunteer**
Start a YouTube channel	**Help an elderly person**
Learn a dance	**Learn a new sport**
Photography	**Learn words in another language**
Gardening	**Learn magic tricks**
Rock climbing	**Sign up for an interest-based class**
Learn to play chess	**Learn to make your favorite meal**
Bowling	
Pottery	

Things I'm going to try:

Try → Notice → Adjust

Step 1: Try
Write down one new thing you want to try this week (big or small).

_____

Step 2: Notice
After you try it, take a moment to reflect

What energized me:
_____

What drained me:
_____

What I learned:
_____

Step 3: Adjust
Use what you noticed to guide your next step

My next step will be:

_____

NOTES:

Reflection
Prompts

What stage do I feel like I'm in right now—exploring, practicing skills, or building toward something bigger?

What stage do I want to grow into next, and what's one action I can take to get there?

What is one habit at school (like showing up on time, staying organized, or preparing for tests) that makes me proud of myself?

How can I strengthen this habit so it continues to help me beyond school?

Think about a time school felt stressful or overwhelming. How did I handle it?

What's one different strategy I could try next time to manage the challenge better?

What skill have I developed in school that I know I'll use in my future (e.g., writing, problem-solving, teamwork)?

How can I practice this skill in a new way to prepare myself for future goals?

Who has supported me in school (parent, teacher, counselor, or mentor), and how did their support make a difference?

How can I remind myself to ask for help earlier next time I face a challenge?

What responsibility at home, work, or volunteering has taught me the most about myself?

How can I take on a new responsibility that challenges me in a positive way?

When have I felt proud of myself for putting in effort, even if the outcome wasn't perfect?

How can I keep focusing on effort and progress instead of just results?

What's one activity or job I tried that didn't fit me, and what did I learn from it?

How can I use what I learned to choose activities or jobs that fit me better in the future?

If I imagine myself five years from now, what kind of person do I want to be?

What small choice can I make this week that will move me closer to that vision?

When I feel pressure to make the "right" choice about my future, what thoughts come up for me?

What encouraging self-talk could I practice to remind myself that growth happens in stages?

What strength do I already use well at school or in work (like leadership, creativity, or persistence)?

How could I use this strength in a new situation to build confidence?

Think of a problem I solved recently. How did I figure it out?

How can I use that same problem-solving strategy in other areas of my life?

SECTION 5 — MEANING & BIG PICTURE

> "The meaning of life is to find your gift. The purpose of life is to give it away." — Pablo Picasso

The Big Picture

Life is not just about the daily ups and downs. It is also about the bigger picture. The core of happiness and life satisfaction comes when you feel connected to something bigger than yourself, have a sense of purpose, values that guide you, and hope for the future. That often means asking some big questions: *Who am I? What do I care about? Where do I fit?*

And here's the thing: it is completely normal to not have all the answers yet. It is also normal to feel disappointed when things do not go the way you hoped. On top of that, the world keeps throwing messages at you, telling you your worth depends on your grades, your appearance, your popularity, or the number of likes you get.

Trying to understand hard emotions can bring up a challenging question:

... and that question can sneak in at different times:

 When you don't get the grade you studied for

 When a friendship drifts apart or you get left out of a group chat

 When you scroll online and compare yourself to the "perfect" people you see

 When you make a mistake and keep replaying it in your head

In those moments, it can feel like the answer is no. But here's the truth: you are not your grades, your looks, or your mistakes. Those things will change over time, but your worth does not.

Shame, Doubt, & Guilt

Sometimes the question "Am I good enough?" shows up as heavy feelings:

Shame says, "I am bad." It attacks who you are and makes you feel like nothing will ever be enough.

Doubt says, "What if I fail? What if people don't like the real me?" It holds you back from trying things that could actually help you grow.

Guilt says, "I did something wrong." A little guilt can point you back to your values, but too much can weigh you down.

Shame can make you feel like something is wrong with *you*, not just something you did. **Doubt** can creep in and make you second-guess your abilities, your choices, or whether you really belong. **Guilt** often shows up when you feel like you let someone down, made a mistake, or didn't live up to your own expectations. These feelings can hurt, but they also reveal what matters most to you: belonging, success, **honesty**, kindness, and responsibility. They are signals, not definitions of your worth.

Instead of asking:

"Am I good enough?"

Ask this instead:

✳ "Good enough for what? Good enough for who?"

✳ "What if I measured myself by my values instead of other people's expectations?"

✳ "If I treated myself like a close friend, what would I say right now?"

> **Let's Reflect: When the question "Am I good enough?" shows up, what is it really pointing to that I care about?**

_____

_____

_____

Choosing Courage and Self-Compassion

When shame, doubt, or guilt show up, you get to choose how to respond. The more you practice courage and compassion, the stronger you get. Small choices every day add up, and they remind you that you can handle way more than you think.

Courage says, "I feel nervous, but I'll show up anyway." Courage might be raising your hand in class even if you are unsure of the answer. It might be trying out for a team, sharing your honest opinion, or walking away from gossip when everyone else is joining in. Sometimes courage is quiet, admitting you need help or letting someone see the real you. Every time you practice courage, you prove that fear does not get to run the show.

Self-compassion says, "I messed up, but that does not make me a mess." It is about being on your own side instead of tearing yourself down. Self-compassion might be changing your self-talk from "I'm such a failure" to "I can learn from this." It might be giving yourself a break when you are tired, writing things down you like about yourself, or catching the mean voice in your head and replacing it with something kinder.

COURAGE

Creating Meaning Through Goals

Meaning does not just fall out of the sky; you build it, step by step. One of the most powerful ways to do that is by setting goals. Goals are not only about achievements like making a team, earning an A, or getting into a certain program. They are also about direction. They give your life something to move toward, especially during seasons when things feel uncertain or confusing.

Whether a goal is big or small, it creates a sense of purpose. A small goal, like committing to practicing a skill a few times a week or showing up consistently even when it's hard, can bring structure and motivation to your days. For example, this might look like setting aside ten minutes to study, exercise, or practice a hobby even when you'd rather scroll on your phone. Bigger goals, like planning for a career or a long-term dream, help you see beyond the present moment. Together, these goals remind you that your efforts matter and that where you are right now is part of a larger story.

Setting goals helps you build confidence in who you are becoming. When you follow through, adjust your plan, or try again after a setback, you learn that you can grow and handle challenges.

Goals give direction when life feels uncertain.

GOAL
SETTING

A goal works best when it is clear and realistic. Think of it like giving yourself a roadmap.

Be Specific

Instead of "I want to do better in school," try, "I'll spend 20 minutes reviewing notes before bed."

Keep It Doable

Pick goals you can actually reach with effort, not ones that feel impossible.

Break It Down

Big goals (like making varsity or getting into college) are built from small steps. Focus on the next step, not the whole mountain.

Stay Flexible

If a goal stops fitting who you are or what you care about, it is okay to adjust. Changing direction is part of growth.

Goal Ideas

 Speak kindly to yourself when you mess up

Try something new this week, even if it makes you nervous

 Reach out to a friend you haven't talked to in a while

Finish a small project or chore without being reminded

 Spend a few minutes reflecting or journaling about your day

Staying Committed to Your Goals

Setting goals is only the first step, following through is where the real growth happens. Here are a few ways to stick with them:

Write Them Down
Putting your goals on paper makes them feel real. You can keep them in a journal or even as a reminder on your phone.

Choose With Care
Ask yourself why the goal matters to you. When you connect it to your values, it is easier to stay motivated.

Track Your Progress
Celebrate small wins along the way. Checking off a step reminds you that progress counts.

Get Support
Share your goal with a friend, coach, or family member who can encourage you and keep you accountable.

Give Yourself Grace
Real progress happens when you stay connected to your goals even after setbacks.

Growing with Your Goals

As you get older, your goals will grow with you. What starts with finishing homework on time can turn into bigger goals like preparing for college, saving money, or learning skills for a future career. Personal goals are also built on each other. Maybe you start with speaking up in class, and over time, that courage grows into leading a group or mentoring someone else.

Each stage of life brings new opportunities to set goals that match where you are and where you are headed. The more you practice setting and sticking to them now, the easier it will be to shape the life you want later.

Contribution & the Bigger Story

Living with purpose is not just about you. It also has to do with the impact you make on the people around you and the way your actions and presence affect a room, a relationship, or a community. **Meaning** often begins to grow when you notice how even small choices, like listening, encouraging someone, or showing up with care when it matters, can make a difference. When you begin to notice how your choices affect others, meaning and purpose feel less like pressure and more like connection..

What is one small goal I'm working on now that could lead to something bigger later?

How Can I Contribute to Make the World a Better Place?

Encouraging a friend who is having a hard day

Helping at home without being asked

Including someone who is being left out

Using your creativity to make something that inspires others

Volunteering for a cause you care about

Why It Matters

Let's take a moment to define what **meaning** really is and why it matters. Meaning comes from living in a way that reflects what you care about most. It shows up when your choices line up with your values, like being honest, speaking up for someone, or doing the right thing even when no one is watching.

Meaning also grows when you discover your strengths and use them in ways that connect you to others or to something bigger than yourself. That might look like supporting a friend, practicing a skill you care about, creating something meaningful, or putting effort into work that matters, even when it goes unnoticed.

How are you already using your abilities or interests in ways that feel important?

My special skills, interests & abilities...

Meaning is not about being happy all the time or having everything figured out. It comes from being true to who you are, building real connections, and having a sense of purpose behind your choices. When life feels chaotic or uncertain, meaning gives you direction.

Challenging moments do not disappear when you live with meaning, but they make more sense. Knowing what matters to you and how you contribute creates **hope**, and hope is what helps you keep moving forward, even when things feel challenging.

What Values Are Important to Me?

Volunteering your time is a way to support others and make a positive difference in your community.

Giving My Time

Taking care of your environment, like picking up trash shows respect for your space.

Respect For My Space

Being a mentor means using your time and attention to support, encourage, and guide someone who looks up to you.

Being A Mentor

Activity: From Values to Vision

In this activity, you'll start by looking through the Values Word Bank and choosing three to five values that feel most important to you right now. The worksheet on the next page already has the first row filled in as an example. There are many values to choose from; the word bank is only a small sample. After reviewing, begin adding your own values in the blank spaces. Write each value in the first column, then set a specific goal that matches this value in the second column. In the third column, imagine your future self if you live by this value and reach your goal.

Once you've filled in your chart, take a moment to read over your answers and notice the connections between your values, goals, and vision. This reflection helps you see how the choices you make today build the future you want. If you run out of space, grab another piece of paper and keep going. Exploring more values over time can give you an even clearer picture of who you are becoming. The purpose of this activity is to help you identify what matters most, turn those values into action through realistic goals, and see the bigger picture of how living out your values shapes the person you're becoming. It's a way to build self-awareness, motivation, and direction as you continue growing into your future self.

Values Word Bank

Adventure   Honesty   Open-   Stability
Authenticity   Integrity   Mindedness   Success
Compassion   Justice   Perseverance   Teamwork
Creativity   Kindness   Respect   Trust
Family   Learning   Security   Wisdom
Freedom   Loyalty   Service   Well-Being
Gratitude   Spirituality

Values	Goals	Future Self
Example: Kindness	Volunteer at an animal shelter	Making a difference

VALUES TO VISION

MAKING A PLAN

This activity will help you practice taking one big idea or goal and breaking it into smaller, more manageable steps.

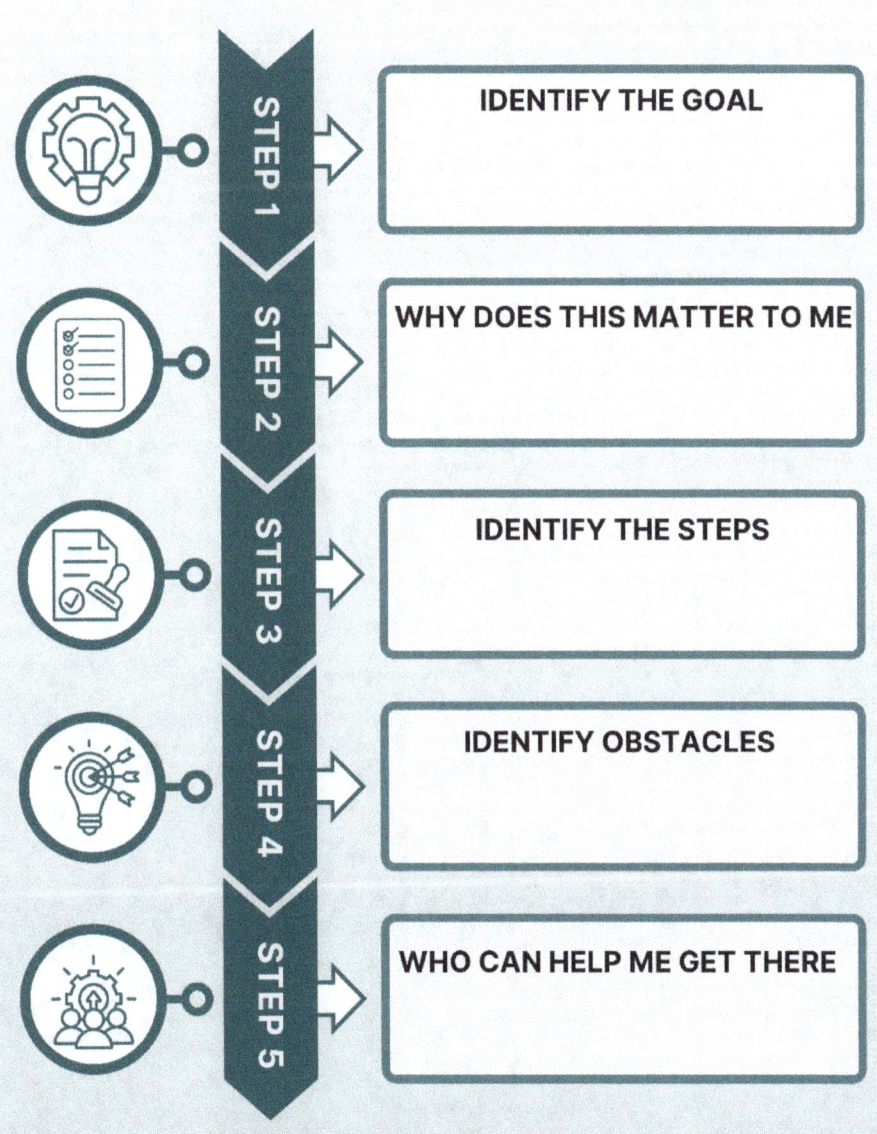

STEP 1 — IDENTIFY THE GOAL

STEP 2 — WHY DOES THIS MATTER TO ME

STEP 3 — IDENTIFY THE STEPS

STEP 4 — IDENTIFY OBSTACLES

STEP 5 — WHO CAN HELP ME GET THERE

NOTES:

Reflection Prompts

Based on the choices I'm making right now, what might my life look like a few years from now?

What do those choices say about who I'm becoming?

When have I felt like I wasn't enough or that something was wrong with me? How did that affect the way I acted around others?

If I could meet that moment with self-compassion instead, what gentle truth could I remind myself of?

What is one area of my life where self-doubt keeps me from speaking up, taking a risk, or showing up as my true self?

What is one small, brave action I can try, even if it feels uncomfortable, that moves me past that doubt?

Think about a person you look up to. This could be
someone you know personally or someone you admire
from a distance. What qualities, values, or behaviors do
they show that stand out to you?
How do they treat others, handle challenges, or stay true
to themselves? Which of those qualities do you want to
carry with you as you grow?

*How can I create more opportunities to show up as that
authentic version of me?*

Think about a recent choice I made. Did I own what happened, or did I put the blame on someone else? What does that show me about the way I handle my choices?

What would it look like to take full responsibility for my choices this week?

What is one mistake or "flaw" I tend to hide from others? What do I fear would happen if people really knew this about me?

What is one way I could practice the "courage to be imperfect" and still show up as myself?

When the future feels uncertain, what do I worry about that's outside my control?

What's one thing I can focus on right now that helps me move forward?

When life has felt "too heavy," what helped me keep going, even if it was just a small thing?

What gives me hope today, and how can I hold onto it when things feel hard again?

When I compare myself to others, how does it influence the choices I make about who I want to become?

What's one way I can focus on my own growth instead of comparison?

Is there guilt I'm carrying (about a friend, my family, school, a mistake I made, or wanting something different) that's holding me back from pursuing what matters to me?

What is one small step I could take toward what matters, even if the guilt doesn't disappear right away?

Life is short, what do I want to be known for by the people who know me now? What would I regret not doing?

What's one small step I can take this week that reflects the way I want people to remember me?

Where do I notice myself making a positive difference, even in small ways?

What is one small way I could contribute to others or the world around me this week?

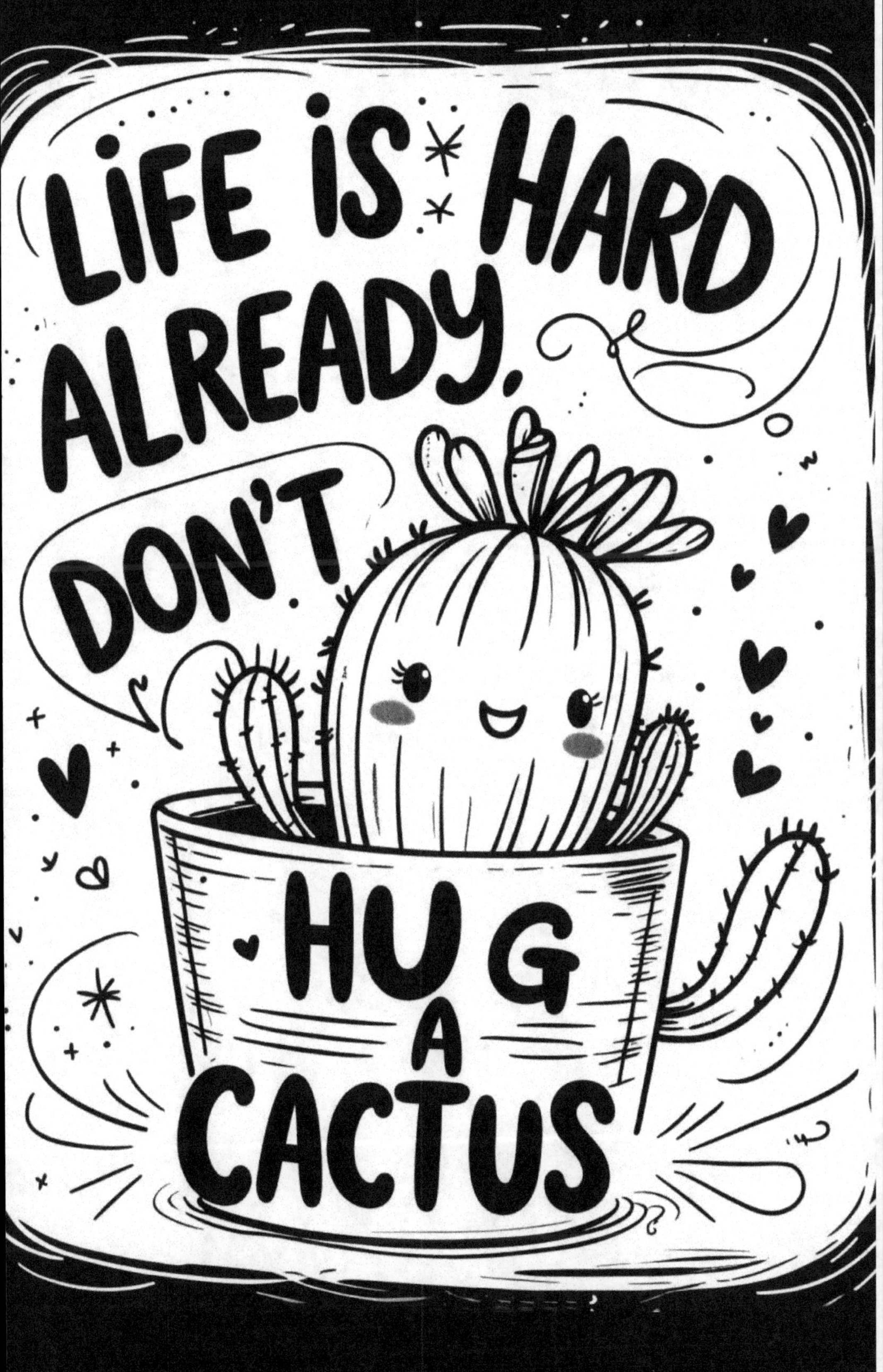
LIFE IS HARD ALREADY.
DON'T
HUG A CACTUS

A Note to End With

By working through this journal, you've done something brave. You've slowed down, reflected, and faced hard questions about who you are and who you're becoming. Along the way, you explored your identity, clarified your values, practiced healthier coping strategies, reflected on friendships and community, considered love and relationships, and envisioned your future. You challenged self-doubt, built courage, and practiced self-compassion.

These pages asked you to dig deep and sit with both the heavy and hopeful parts of your story. Life will always bring storms, but now you've built tools to navigate them: self-awareness, resilience, and a vision for the future. When you look back, remember these accomplishments are not just words on paper. They are evidence of your courage and reminders that you are capable of facing whatever comes next.

On the next page, you'll find your final activity: writing a letter to yourself. This is your chance to gather what you've learned, speak to yourself with kindness, and create words you can return to when life feels heavy. Think of it as a gift for your future self—a reminder that you are capable, resilient, and worthy of love and hope.

This isn't the end. It's a new beginning.

Final Activity: Letter to Myself

Write a letter to yourself that you can return to in moments of doubt or struggle. Speak with kindness and compassion, reminding yourself of your strengths, the challenges you've overcome, and the words you most need to hear. Let this letter hold the encouragement and hope you wish someone would give you. Keep it in your journal as a reminder that you are capable, resilient, and worthy—always.

_____

_____

_____

_____

_____

_____

_____

_____

Key Ideas
&
Their Meaning

Key Ideas and Their Meaning

The words and ideas in this section are not strict dictionary definitions. Instead, they reflect how these ideas show up throughout this journal — in stories, examples, activities, and reflection questions. Each meaning is based on how the concept is explored across different sections, not on one single definition. Use this as a guide to better understand what each idea means *in the context of your own life and this journal.*

Anxiety
Anxiety is that uneasy, nervous feeling that shows up when you're worried about what might happen next. It can feel like racing thoughts, a tight chest, or trouble relaxing. Anxiety often appears when something matters to you, like friendships, school, or being accepted.

Belonging
Belonging is the feeling of being accepted and valued for who you truly are. It's about feeling like you matter and that there's a place where you fit, whether that's with friends, family, a team, or a community. Real belonging doesn't require you to change yourself or pretend; it grows when you feel safe being real.

Burnout
Burnout happens when you're tired not just in your body, but in your motivation and emotions too. It can come from constant pressure, stress, or feeling like you have to keep pushing without

rest. Burnout is a sign that something needs to change, not that you're weak.

Comparison

Comparison is when you measure yourself against others, often through social media, grades, looks, or popularity. It usually leads to feeling "not enough." Your worth isn't based on how you stack up to someone else.

Confidence

Confidence isn't about being loud or perfect. It's about trusting yourself and believing you can handle what comes your way. Confidence grows when you try, learn, and keep going, not when you never mess up.

Courage

Courage means choosing to show up even when something feels uncomfortable or scary. It might look like speaking up, setting a boundary, trying again after failure, or being honest about your feelings. Courage doesn't mean fear disappears; it means you move forward anyway.

Disappointment

Disappointment is the feeling that comes when things don't turn out the way you hoped. It can hurt, especially when you worked hard or cared deeply. Disappointment is part of growth and doesn't mean you failed; it means you tried.

Emotional Awareness

Emotional awareness is the ability to notice and name what you're feeling. Instead of ignoring emotions or letting them explode, emotional awareness helps you understand what your feelings are trying to tell you. This skill makes coping, communication, and self-compassion easier.

Emotional Safety

Emotional safety means feeling safe to be yourself without fear of being mocked, ignored, or punished for your feelings. In emotionally safe relationships, you can be honest, set boundaries, and trust that you'll be respected. Emotional safety is a foundation for healthy love and friendship.

Empathy

Empathy is the ability to understand and care about how someone else feels. It doesn't mean fixing their problems; it means listening and showing compassion. Empathy strengthens friendships and helps build trust and connection.

Fear

Fear is a natural response to uncertainty or risk. It often shows up when you're about to try something new or vulnerable. Fear doesn't mean stop, it often means something matters.

Grief

Grief is the pain that comes from loss, change, or disappointment. It doesn't only happen when someone dies, it can also come from losing friendships, routines, or expectations. Grief is not something to rush through; it's something to move through with care and support.

Guilt

Guilt shows up when you feel you've done something wrong or hurt someone. It can be helpful if it leads to repair and growth, but heavy guilt can keep you stuck.

Hope

Hope is the belief that things can get better, even when life feels heavy. It doesn't mean everything is perfect; it means you believe your efforts matter. Hope grows through small steps, support, and meaning.

Identity

Identity is how you see yourself and the story you tell about who you are. It includes your values, interests, personality, experiences, and goals. Identity isn't fixed; it grows and changes as you learn more about yourself.

Insecurity

Insecurity is the feeling of not being good enough or worrying about how others see you. It can show up in comparison, people-pleasing, or self-doubt.

Intuition

Intuition is your inner sense or "gut feeling" that helps you recognize when something feels right or off. It often shows up through your body or emotions before you can explain it with words. Learning to listen to intuition helps you make healthier choices.

Loneliness

Loneliness is the feeling of being emotionally disconnected, even when you're not physically alone. It's a signal that you need connection, not proof that something is wrong with you.

Motivation

Motivation is the energy or desire to take action, like studying, practicing a skill, or trying again after a setback. It naturally rises and falls, especially when life feels stressful or overwhelming.

Overwhelm

Overwhelm happens when everything feels like too much at once. Your thoughts, emotions, or responsibilities may pile up. This journal helps you slow down, break things into smaller steps, and regain a sense of control.

Purpose

Purpose is the sense that your life has meaning and direction. It comes from living in a way that reflects your values and strengths. Purpose doesn't require having everything figured out, it grows through choices, effort, and connection.

Resilience

Resilience is the ability to keep going after setbacks. It's not about being tough all the time, it's about learning, adjusting, and trying again. Every time you bounce back, resilience grows.

Self-Compassion

Self-compassion means responding to yourself with kindness when you make a mistake or struggle, instead of being harsh or mean to yourself. It looks like acknowledging that everyone messes up and allowing yourself to learn without tearing yourself down.

Self-Doubt

Self-doubt is the inner voice that makes you question your abilities or whether you are good enough. It can cause you to hesitate, stay quiet, or avoid trying because you're afraid of getting it wrong.

Self-Respect

Self-respect means believing your needs, feelings, and boundaries matter. It shows up in how you talk to yourself and what treatment you accept from others. Self-respect is a foundation for healthy relationships.

Shame

Shame is the painful belief that something is wrong with you as a person, not just that you made a mistake. It can show up as wanting to hide, stay quiet, or pull away from others. Shame often makes people feel small, unworthy, or afraid of being judged.

Stress

Stress is your body's response to pressure or demands. It can show up as a racing heart, tense muscles, headaches, stomach discomfort, trouble sleeping, or feeling on edge. Some stress is normal and can help you focus, but too much stress over time can affect your mood, energy, and health.

Survival Moves

Survival moves are habits you pick up to protect yourself during hard or stressful situations. This can look like staying quiet to avoid conflict, putting others first to keep the peace, or acting tough to hide hurt. These behaviors helped you get through something difficult, even if they don't always help you now.

Trust

Trust means believing in yourself and allowing others to earn access to your inner world. It grows slowly through honesty, consistency, and boundaries. Trust is key to feeling safe and connected.

Vulnerability

Vulnerability is the courage to be real, even when it feels risky. It might mean sharing feelings, asking for help, or being honest. Vulnerability strengthens connection and builds deeper trust.

Worth

Worth is the value you have as a person, even on days when you mess up, fall behind, or don't feel confident. It doesn't go up when you get good grades or attention, and it doesn't drop when you fail, get rejected, or feel left out. In this journal, worth shows up in moments like choosing to keep going after a hard day, setting a boundary when something feels wrong, or speaking to yourself with kindness instead of criticism. Your worth stays the same, even when your life feels confusing or unfinished.

DREAM...

CREATE...